Lachlan Macquarie
from Mull to Australia

by
Fiona Marsden

Illustrations by Fiona Marsden and Pat James

Brown & Whittaker

2001

Acknowledgements

I am particularly grateful to the staff of Mull Museum library and to Bruce McQuarrie of the Clan MacQuarrie Association for much practical help and encouragement in the gathering of information for this booklet; to Jo Currie for useful discussion and criticism; to Jamie Howard for the wide ranging access he allows visitors to Ulva, and to Claire Barlow for information on Inchkenneth.

Ted Brockie kindly photographed the estate plan of Jarvisfield from the original in Mull Museum, which also supplied the plan of Ormaig and the photograph of Macquarie's statue. The four portrait sketches of members of Macquarie's family on pages 7, 8, 11 and 16 are based on miniatures in the Mitchell Library, State Library of New South Wales, and that of Elizabeth Macquarie on page 12 is based on a portrait attributed to Richard Read the elder in the Tasmanian Museum and Art Gallery, Hobart. The sketch of the last MacQuarrie chief is based on a copy in Duart Castle of a lost portrait. The silhouette of Lachlan Macquarie, junior, and the medicine chest are in a private collection. The commemorative silver "dollar & dump", minted in 1988, in the possession of Ulva Ferry Primary School was kindly made available for the illustration on page 18. The cover portrait of Lachlan Macquarie as Assistant Adjutant-General for the London Military District by John Opie (1805) is reproduced by kind permission of the Mitchell Library, State Library of New South Wales.

ISBN 0 9532775 7 7

Published by Brown & Whittaker Publishing, Tobermory, Isle of Mull, PA75 6PR
www.brown-whittaker.co.uk

Set in Times New Roman and printed in Fort William, Scotland
by Nevisprint Ltd

From Mull to Australia

Escape from Poverty

Lachlan Macquarie was born on 31st January 1761. His birthplace is unknown but assumed to be Ulva, much the largest of the little islands scattered off Mull's Atlantic coast. The name Ulva, came from the Old Norse Ulf-eyr, meaning wolf island, but these were possibly human wolves, the ferocious forebears of the clan MacQuarrie, of mixed Nordic and Celtic stock. By Lachlan's day, interclan raiding had finally ceased and people were struggling to survive on insufficient farms. Like most of Europe, Mull and Ulva were becoming overpopulated, but clan chiefs whose status once depended on the fighting men they could muster, still liked to cram their followers onto tiny subdivided holdings. Such traditions were slow to break down, but the landless and ambitious were increasingly migrating to the growing towns of mainland Britain, going for soldiers in British and foreign wars or sailing for the New World where land grants were available to settlers.

Nothing is known for certain of Lachlan's home on Ulva but at Ormaig, his probable birthplace, roofless cottages survive among sparse fields and travellers crossing the island were dismayed at the poverty they found there. From 1775, Macquarie's family rented one sixth of a little farm at Oskamull, next door to Lachlan's sister and husband, Farquhar Maclaine, on the Mull mainland. Lachlan's father, also Lachlan Macquarie, is said to have been the last miller at nearby Lagganulva. Other accounts call him a blacksmith, house carpenter or drover who walked local cattle to distant English markets. He was probably all these things, since travellers stressed the lack of skill among Highland craftsmen forced to turn their hands to many occupations in order to earn some sort of living. Family tradition described him as an active, good-looking young man, but he died of a lung disease just after the move to Oskamull. He was buried in Kilvickewen cemetery on Ulva with two infant sons. For some years the family could afford no stone to commemorate him.

Lachlan MacQuarrie, 16th and last Chief of MacQuarrie

3

In addition to his daughter, Elizabeth, there were four surviving sons: Hector, Donald, Lachlan and Charles, the youngest by ten years. Both parents were cousins of sorts to the 16th and last chief of the MacQuarries, but local leading families were as little able to adapt to difficult times as their clansmen and were slipping into poverty. MacQuarrie of Ulva was bankrupted by his creditors and lost the lands on which his title depended in 1777. The family connections of Lachlan's mother, Margaret, were more useful. Her grandfather had been 12th clan chieftain of the Maclaines of Lochbuie on Mull. Her brother Murdoch Maclaine unexpectedly succeeded as 19th Maclaine of Lochbuie in 1785 after several cousins had died off and the quarrelsome 18th chief, his friend Archibald Maclaine, was killed in a shipboard fracas.

The Lochbuie estates were almost as encumbered by debts as those of the old chief MacQuarrie, but Murdoch had served, when he could, as an army officer and betweenwhiles traded as an Edinburgh merchant. He and his first wife brought Lachlan and Charles to Edinburgh and provided them with an education to enable them too to become army officers. They received basic instruction in reading, writing, arithmetic and essential standard English, since both were Gaelic speakers.

The Highland regiments for which they were destined were an invaluable financial lifeline for impoverished local families. Founded soon after the disastrous defeat of Bonnie Prince Charlie at Culloden in 1746, they were intended to realign Highlanders' loyalties to the British crown and to disperse their warlike energies abroad. Substantial fortunes could be made overseas, especially in India, and officers' commissions were much sought after, but had to be purchased. Only in times of national emergency and rapid recruitment could junior commissions be obtained more easily by those with the right contacts.

The American War of Independence proved such an opportunity in 1775 and following years. Both the bankrupt MacQuarrie chief, aged over 60 and Lachlan at the age of 16 secured lieutenant's commissions. Since Murdoch Maclaine's mercantile experience had been of use to the army in the purchase of supplies, he was allowed to nominate several boys as junior officers. Lachlan and a 13 year old Hector Maclean sailed to Canada among this group in 1776. Their ship, the *Newcastle Jane* was attacked by an American privateer, but fought it off successfully under Maclaine's command as Lachlan and another boy loaded the heavy guns below deck. He received half a guinea prize money.

Lachlan saw no further action in seven years' service, but soon after arrival in Halifax, Nova Scotia, he received a promised commission as an ensign in the 84th Regiment. Five months later, he was promoted to lieutenant and in 1781, he transferred to the 71st Highland Regiment and moved south to serve in America. In 1783, he was posted to Jamaica and in 1784 he returned home. These were useful years for making contacts and learning army accountancy, a profitable sideline through which Murdoch Maclaine had been able to add to his earnings. Regimental pay-rolls could be invested for personal profit until needed to pay the troops and buying army supplies offered similar opportunities. These arrangements were commonplace and acceptable as long as the operators did not overstep the mark or get caught doing so. So great, however, was the scale of profiteering from army contracts during the American war, that such activities came to be regarded much more critically. The capable General Cornwallis, who was let down by more senior officers and whose surrender at Yorktown sealed the British defeat, was particularly active in cracking down on abuses. On return to Mull, Maclaine got drawn into a network of enquiries and Lachlan, who had kept his military paybooks for some months, was sent to London to give evidence. Lachlan's book-keeping had been impeccable but others' had been chaotic, money was unaccounted for and his uncle remained under a cloud.

From 1785, Lachlan worked as Murdoch Maclaine's factor on the newly inherited Lochbuie estates but, though very fortunate in his job, he was inclined to consider it a stop-gap. As all former officers continued to receive half-pay, he could afford a servant and hoped for a commission in the East Indies. Mull offered only a drab existence after the good company, diversions and comforts of military life behind the lines, but his older brothers' experience of the war had been much grimmer. Both seem to have gone out as volunteers and both were captured. After two years among the squalors of an American prisoner-of-war camp, Hector had died of the same lung complaint that killed his father. The second brother, Donald returned from a French prisoner-of-war camp simple-minded and of little use around the farm.

In 1787, when four regiments were being raised to counter French threats to Britain's lucrative trading interests in the East, Lachlan was sponsored by General Allan Maclean of Torloisk, whose roots were on Mull and who was credited with saving Canada for Britain in the American war. This time the commission had to be earned and he was required to raise at least fifteen new recruits for the 77th Regiment bound for India. Memories of war casualties in America may have been too fresh or poverty on Mull and Ulva not yet sufficiently severe to tempt able-bodied men into hazardous foreign service as private soldiers. He tramped vainly through Mull and the neighbouring mainland, but only Murdoch MacQuarrie, the 16 year old son of the ruined MacQuarrie of Ulva was prepared to go with him in hope of becoming an officer.

Finally, Lachlan filled his quota from among the unemployed and destitute of Glasgow's growing slums. They were shipped to London and marched to Kent to join the Regiment for embarkation at Deal. Here, four of the contingent of twenty-one were dismissed as unfit, he forfeited their recruiting costs and received a chilly welcome from his commanding officer who had been led to expect a hundred recruits.

The Wealth of India

After four months at sea, Macquarie's regiment reached Bombay in August 1788. He found the heat and noisy crowds oppressive and was unimpressed by the scruffy buildings. Mosquitoes swarming in from neighbouring swamps made kilts impossible. The connection with malaria had not been recognised and there was an enormous death-toll among Europeans from unfamiliar tropical diseases but these risks were acceptable to those coming to India intent on making their fortunes.

Over the past two hundred years, the East India Company, in seeking to protect its trading posts, had grown into a dominant military power, controlling most of the territory formerly ruled by the collapsing Moghul empire. Counter-balancing French influence had been crushed and punitive levels of taxation imposed on the Indian population. Military force was also effective in extorting favourable trading terms for the Company and its employees whose widespread private trading began to undermine Company profits and government revenue. Finally, public resentment in Britain at the splendour in which returning Company officials, the nabobs (Indian princes), could afford to live and the bitter complaints of real Indian princes provoked reforms.

Two years before Macquarie's arrival, the great reformer Warren Hastings, the first Governor General of India, had fallen victim to the competing interests of those demanding profits and those opposed to the East India Company on principle. Hastings was impeached in Parliament on trumped up charges and took many years to clear his name. Such were the hazards faced by administrators of distant territories who worked contrary to local vested interests at a time of rapid colonial expansion, as Macquarie would one day learn to his cost. Meanwhile, as a young man fresh to India, he shared the dreams of those who assumed they could make a quick fortune and retire home early to a country estate.

He was soon disillusioned. Lord Cornwallis, scourge of profiteers from the American war, was now Governor General of India and stringent reductions in army allowances came into force within two months of Macquarie's arrival. Another result of the British defeat in America was an overhaul of army training and tactics, which kept junior officers very busy drilling troops in tedious new manoeuvres. Meanwhile administrative reform left few opportunities for real fighting. Macquarie had missed the great days of military conquest and lucrative share-outs of prize money.

More rewarding were promotions gained by tireless courting of the powerful and well-connected. Naturally energetic, convivial and eager to please, Macquarie was popular on Bombay's small social scene where organising entertainments was an excellent way of getting noticed. Within months he had outstripped more senior lieutenants to become a captain and, by late 1790, he was beginning to boost his earnings through military paymasterships. With like-minded officers, he ran risks to speculate advantageously with regimental pay rolls and on at least one occasion had to extricate himself in a panic when the more dubious of these activities came close to discovery. Standards in public life were growing stiffer.

He welcomed opportunities for active service when they did arise. In 1790 and 91, very soon after the French Revolution, moves were made against Tipu, Sultan of Mysore, in southern India, who had entered into an anti-British conspiracy with the Revolutionaries. Macquarie proved a brave and capable soldier when his health allowed, but field conditions were appalling. Stores and heavy guns had to be hauled through tropical jungles and mountainous terrain. Premature monsoon rains brought icy plunges in temperature and guns, equipment, men and draught animals were lost in churning mud and flooded rivers. Stragglers were harried and cut down by elusive jungle fighters. From these and lesser campaigns, Macquarie struggled home ever more prostrate with fevers, but gradually rewards from looted palaces and captured treasuries in addition to his pay and profits from handling regimental funds enabled him to build up a satisfying reserve of capital.

Almost from his arrival in India, he had been sending money to Mull to help his mother and sister on their tiny farms. To assist his brother Charles, now the Lochbuie factor, in escaping such a life, he bought him an army commission and sent the fare for India, but, to his disgust, Charles had other ideas and transferred to a British-based regiment with better opportunities. Macquarie had been quick to pay off debts to Murdoch Maclaine, incurred while kitting himself out and recruiting for India, but soon their relationship shifted. Maclaine's plans for improving his estate had been thwarted by family debts and intrigue and he had indulged himself with a new mansion. As the money slipped through his uncle's fingers, Macquarie became the benefactor, concerned for the education and prospects of Maclaine's rapidly growing family, especially the daughters whose interests were often overlooked.

As well as money, there were presents. For his aunt Maclaine, Macquarie sought out one of the most costly of Indian shawls. Their swirling patterns and rich colours had become highly fashionable and the Paisley textile industry, just outside Glasgow, would soon make its name producing machine-made copies. Macquarie's mother and sister received plainer shawls and all his female cousins came to expect gifts of intricate Indian craftsmanship very different from functional Highland products. Not only Macquarie but a host of other soldiers and adventurers from across Scotland were sending home money and presents to those living pinched lives and encouraging relatives to seek opportunities in a much wider world. Meanwhile, outsiders, newly rich with Indian and other fortunes, were buying their way into estates whose traditional owners, like the chief of the MacQuarries, had failed.

young Jane Jarvis

A decisive change in Macquarie's life and outlook followed his marriage in 1793. His wife, Jane Jarvis, was the heiress daughter of a former Chief Justice of Antigua. She was far above Macquarie in rank and fortune and had come to India with her sister and wealthy brother-in-law, James Morley, who had grown rich in the service of the East India Company. He was now a Director. Jane had had much better offers, but her family reluctantly agreed to her marriage with Macquarie once he had worked hard at his contacts to earn promotion to brigade major. Her money was placed out of his reach in a trust fund and, as a gesture of good-will, he added his own savings to it.

Jane Jarvis

At first, the hospitality expected of a married officer and the house, carriage, silverware and servants appropriate to his wife's status plunged Macquarie seriously into debt. Only a welcome move away from fashionable Bombay to the quiet backwater of Calicut, where his regiment was posted, enabled the couple to live comfortably within their means and recoup their losses. They named their new home Staffa Lodge after the beautiful Hebridean island that had grown famous just as it slipped from the MacQuarrie clan's possession. As evidence of pedigree, Macquarie borrowed the coat of arms of his dispossessed chief to emblazon on carriage doors and engrave on his silver.

Poor Jane was no soldier's wife. She was pretty and animated, but also dependent and clinging. She suffered badly when her sister's family left India and she could not cope with Macquarie's absences on campaign. They both looked forward to retiring soon to a Mull estate, once he felt he could afford it. In 1795, Macquarie took part in an expedition to force the surrender of Ceylon into British safe-keeping, ostensibly on behalf of the Dutch royal family which had been replaced by a revolutionary government. He returned to find Jane elated by an imaginary pregnancy but in fact seriously ill with tuberculosis. She died on a recuperative voyage to China less than three years after their marriage.

Macquarie plunged into a depression that overshadowed his next five years in India. Jane's money had left him relatively wealthy but retirement without her had little appeal. He preferred the diversions of military campaigns, which continued to undermine his health and his career faltered. Though he resented his lack of promotion, he was no longer willing to exert himself or to pay for more senior commissions, which was the accepted route to advancement. Instead, he devoted himself to improving the lot of others. Family slaves in Antigua and India were freed and others, who enjoyed security as family servants, were given an education. Junior commissions were offered to a wider circle of connections including youngsters from unrelated but deserving families on Mull. If necessary, he would pay for their schooling. Murdoch Maclaine's daughters received money on marriage and there were further gifts for his own and Jane's family, including a regular income for his mother and war-damaged brother Donald.

Finally, renewed family contact restored a sense of purpose to Macquarie's life and helped lift his depression. After the final Mysore campaign resulted in the defeat and death of Tipu in 1799, Macquarie's regiment was sent to help prevent Napoleon's seizure of Egypt as a springboard for India. Despite misgivings of the future Duke of Wellington over Macquarie's health and his indecision over his career, he was given a prestigious administrative post as Deputy Adjutant-General to the entire force. It arrived too late for the fighting, but suffered heavy casualties from an ill-considered desert march and bubonic plague. Macquarie himself nearly died from a burst blood vessel. Meanwhile, his brother Charles, in Egypt with the Black Watch regiment, had narrowly escaped death when shot through the face at Aboukir Bay where the French invasion fleet was destroyed. The brothers were able to spend two companionable months together after thirteen years apart.

By now, Murdoch Maclaine's financial situation was getting desperate and part of the Lochbuie estate had to be sold to satisfy creditors. Some years earlier, Macquarie had given him a reluctant promise to invest in land on Mull and now he was persuaded by Charles to purchase 10,000 of their uncle's forfeit acres. It was a much larger property than he had envisaged, but it gave him a stake in the future and a reason for returning home. His land cost £10,060 out of a total fortune of £20,000 while Charles received £2000 to help purchase an estate of his own.

The Absentee Landlord

After further service in Egypt and a brief return to India to order his affairs, Macquarie reached England in 1802. He was still a serving officer and the threat of a French invasion prevented him from going immediately to Scotland. Instead he was swept into an agreeable whirl of high society while a welcome appointment as Assistant Adjutant-General for the London district brought further contacts with nobility and royalty. In addition to official duties, he pulled strings, not always successfully, to place five more aspiring lieutenants from Mull and to further the careers of his brother and brother-in-law, George Jarvis. He even angled for a military sinecure to provide an income for the former chief of the MacQuarries, now aged 87 and struggling in poverty.

Only in 1804, could he obtain two month's leave to travel to Mull. He arrived to find Murdoch Maclaine on his death-bed and spent a few final days with him before proceeding to Oskamull to break the news to his mother. He had neither seen nor written to her for over sixteen years, confining himself to messages sent in letters to others, since Gaelic was then an oral culture. The unfortunate Donald had died in 1801 and old Mrs Macquarie worried constantly about her surviving soldier sons but they now lived in very different worlds. Macquarie spent only two nights at her little cottage and otherwise rode over from his base at Lochbuie. During the visit, he arranged for improvements and enlargements to be made to her home, he engaged two servants to help with farm work and ensured that Murdoch Maclaine's widow would order comforts for her that were unobtainable on Mull.

On 16th July, the anniversary of Jane's death, he and Charles ceremonially took possession of their new properties. Macquarie's stretched across the narrow isthmus linking north and south Mull but he could not shift a sitting tenant by the eastern shore at Callachally, where he had dreamed of building a grand new house overlooking the Sound of Mull. Instead, he settled on a site at Gruline, on the north west tip of Loch Ba. Both house and estate were to be named Jarvisfield in Jane's memory. Travelling across the Highlands for pleasure the following month, he found a model for his planned new house in General Grant's fine mansion at Ballindalloch, in Strathspey. Charles' smaller property joined Jarvisfield at the Forsa river at Pennygown and took its name, Glenforsa, from the whole valley of which it formed the eastern half.

To Macquarie an estate was of little value without an heir. While in India, he had thought fondly of Jane's widowed sister Dorothea Morley as a possible wife, but in London he found she had grown stout in the intervening years. Now his considered choice fell on Elizabeth Campbell, the 27 year old sister-in-law of the late Murdoch Maclaine. She had no money and lacked Jane's good looks, but he admired her management of the Lochbuie household during his uncle's difficult last days and he had been impressed by garden designs she created for her family home at Airds, where he stayed on his journey north. When he met up with her at Inveraray to return to London, he found her good company and a resilient traveller. She was a granddaughter of Archibald Campbell of Stonefield, Chamberlain of Argyll, who had supervised the building of the third Duke of Argyll's famous castle and model town at Inveraray. An aunt was the mother of Lord Breadalbane, and had helped introduce Macquarie into London society.

Macquarie mused in his diary that Elizabeth would make a good wife for a soldier, but her contacts and interests made her quite as useful to someone with a new estate to develop. He proposed hurriedly when it became clear that he must return to India and she agreed to wait for him since he had sworn at Jane's death never to expose another wife to that unhealthy environment.

His unwelcome return to Bombay resulted from the exposure of two military protégées as mere ten-year-old boys who had been drawing half-pay in Scotland since the age of five. Macquarie had guaranteed that they had reached the minimum age for a commission, which was 16. One was Charles' illegitimate son Hector and the other was Murdoch Maclaine's second son John. It was a commonplace scam, but the intensification of the Napoleonic wars was resulting in far too many juvenile lieutenants being unmasked when summoned for active service. Only the exceptionally well-connected could still get away with such practices.

Elizabeth Henrietta Macquarie, née Campbell

Soon after reaching India, Macquarie learnt that the promotion to lieutenant-colonel that he had been agitating for, had been granted, though rather pointedly in the 73rd Regiment which had just sailed for England. By then he had met the expenses of travelling out and re-equipping himself and had also made a commitment to work for Jonathan Duncan, the Governor of Bombay, from whom he had earlier gained valuable administrative experience. A member of the Governor's circle and close friend of Macquarie's was Charles Forbes, a textile merchant and financier whose philanthropy, political views and racial tolerance had helped shape Macquarie's social conscience. Forbes also looked after his money. On the fringes of the group was a disputatious philosopher, Sir James Mackintosh, who was briefly in Bombay as a judge, in the unrealised hope of earning a lot of money. He was already taking a critical interest in the poor management of Britain's troubled penal settlement at Botany Bay. Macquarie settled comfortably back into this familiar world among his fellow Scots and had saved another £3000 before a certain frostiness on Elizabeth's part made him exert himself to return home. He left India for good in March 1807, carrying confidential despatches on a risky journey across Persia and Russia.

He married Elizabeth quietly in November, within days of his return, and they soon joined his 73rd Regiment at Perth. Here, Sir James Drummond, another wealthy friend and mentor from India, was now a member of parliament. In August 1808, the Macquaries visited Mull and arrangements were made to transform the unproductive wetlands of Salen, at the eastern edge of Jarvisfield, into a model village after the current fashion. A factor was appointed to run Glenforsa and Jarvisfield estates, to pay Macquarie's mother and sister an allowance from the rents and to oversee developments at Salen. The following month, Elizabeth's first child, Jane Jarvis Macquarie, was born in Perth, but survived only until December.

After so many years service in India, Macquarie was confident of a long stay in Britain, particularly since his regiment was badly in need of recruitment and training to bring it up to strength. Instead, he was shocked to learn in December 1808, that he was to be "transported" as Lieutenant Governor to New South Wales, where he and his regiment were required to restore order after a mutinous uprising.

Such a posting, to a distant and insignificant backwater, was deeply unpopular at a time when glory and promotion could be won on the battlefields of Europe. With this in mind, the intended Governor, Brigadier Miles Nightingall, haggled unsuccessfully for more generous terms, then reported sick, leaving Lieutenant-Colonel Macquarie to lobby for the Governor's post himself. For lack of better candidates, he got it, learning of his appointment less than a month before he and Elizabeth set sail on 22 May 1809. He was to be promoted to full colonel on arrival.

Transported to New South Wales

Almost forty years earlier, in 1770, the explorer Captain Cook had made an unexpected landfall on Australia's eastern coast and claimed a long stretch of it for Britain. He named this New South Wales. In those days, the main Australian landmass was known as New Holland, after tentative Dutch exploration, but no territorial claims had been made because of uncertainties in navigation. Cook was confident of finding it again after recent British advances in plotting longitude, whilst dietary experiments, including the use of limes, had proved effective in preventing his crews from dying of scurvy, through vitamin deficiency on so long a voyage. Even so, no return visit was made to this near inaccessible territory for almost eighteen years. By then, overcrowding in Britain's gaols had reached crisis point. Convicts could no longer be sent to the lost American colonies and volatile concentrations of prisoners were as unwelcome in other British settlements overseas as they were at home. New South Wales seemed the only solution.

Elizabeth, Macquarie's second wife

In 1788, the eleven ships of the First Fleet arrived at Cook's old anchorage, Botany Bay, in remarkably good order after more than eight months at sea. They carried about 1500 people of whom 736 were convicts, with three companies of marines to guard them, and some accompanying women and children. Poor survival skills, starvation, drought, floods and unscheduled arrivals of fresh shiploads of convicts repeatedly brought their fragile settlement close to disaster. A succession of short-stay naval Governors gradually lost control of the marines and a special New South Wales Corps sent out to replace them. Soon, army officers, who dominated the judicial system, were running the colony much to their own advantage. They enforced the use of rum as a cash currency, since real money was in short supply, then encouraged alcoholism and enriched themselves with huge surcharges on all imports of rum and most other necessities entering the colony.

Eventually, in 1806, the disciplinarian Captain Bligh, who had won public admiration for his heroic voyage in an open boat after the mutiny on the Bounty and had later faced down naval mutineers at the Nore, was sent to restore order. It was a disaster. He was quickly deposed by a mutinous coalition of army officers and influential settlers and retreated to live on board ship.

This was the situation Macquarie was sent to resolve. He was prepared for armed resistance, but spring floods, impending famine and collapsed morale had done their work and he received a sincere welcome when he landed to be declared Governor on 1st January 1810. A much-needed grain ship providentially arrived two weeks later. His official mission was reconciliation. Any judicial proceedings were to take place in London and the ring-leaders had already left to put their case. Bligh and others, prominent in the dispute, soon followed, taking witnesses with them. The infamous New South Wales Corps, the "Rum Corps" was replaced by Macquarie's own 73rd Regiment, but those who chose to remain as settlers received land grants and others stayed on as a veteran corps. Macquarie's determination to let bygones be bygones in this and other respects was to set up an undertow of resentment among those who had suffered under the rebellious regime, while the exodus of those involved in earlier administrations forced him into a reliance on convicts and former convicts which would upset other susceptibilities. At the time, these seemed transient difficulties.

Following his instructions, Macquarie set about improving the moral tone of the colony as energetically as he had once drilled slack regiments into shape. He urged marriage on cohabiting couples, stressed Sunday observance and enforced church parades on all convicts. He closed three-quarters of the taverns, whittled away at the destructive reliance on rum and was personally convinced that a better civic tone would do much to improve the community's self-respect. He insisted that the straggle of dilapidated buildings that made up the core settlement at Sydney should be rebuilt along proper streets. Gardens were to be fenced, livestock controlled, laundering banned from the brook and nude bathing from the quay. Messy industries were removed from the town centre, roads built to outlying settlements, and night watches and a civic police force established. Imposing public buildings were planned and the first free schools set up for poor children. Respect for aborigines and their culture was actively promoted.

By now, New South Wales held over 10,000 Europeans. The settled territory covered almost 2,500 square miles on the mainland with further communities spread thinly across Van Diemen's Land (Tasmania), the great island to the south. On other isolated islands, recalcitrant convicts endured hard labour under brutal conditions. Macquarie and Elizabeth toured widely. He inspected agricultural progress, took measures to limit flood damage, built up government stores to ward off starvation and laid out neat new townships. Wherever he went anonymous landmarks were named after his political and Colonial Office masters, himself, his family, his officials and his Scottish homeland. To underline the importance of the Governor's office, he travelled in style with a coach and coachman, a purpose-built boat, sumptuous Indian campaign tents and a retinue of officials. Such statements had been important in India, but were less well understood in frontier towns and government departments seeking to economise.

Having got to grips with the more pressing problems of New South Wales in his first year, Macquarie was feeling pleased with progress midway through his second. This was about the time it took for reports and financial accounts to reach London and re-actions of the Colonial Office to be relayed back, with a certain amount of administrative delay in between. Macquarie was ill-prepared for a blast of official disapproval from the new Colonial Secretary, Lord Liverpool. The main problem was his expenditure, but by the time he had replied to these strictures, Lord Liverpool had become prime minister and was replaced by the more tactful and supportive Lord Bathurst. Macquarie felt able to continue on his relatively free-spending way, confident of better understanding once his policies were fully explained. Promotion to brigadier-general in 1811 and major-general in 1813 seemed to signal official approval but disruptive time-lags continued to bedevil his contacts with London and contributed to his lack of awareness of the changing political climate during his twelve years as Governor.

Modern monument to Macquarie in Sydney, Australia.
Plinth

HIS GENIUS FOR ADMINISTRATION
AND CONCEPT OF THE FUTURE OF THE COLONY
LED TO CONSIDERABLE DEVELOPMENT
IN ORGANISED FINANCE
PUBLIC WORKS AND MANUFACTURING
INLAND EXPLORATION AND SETTLEMENT
FINE ARCHITECTURE
AND PATRONAGE OF THE ARTS AND LITERATURE

The cost of his administration proved an enduring difficulty, largely because of an enormous increase in the number of transported convicts, who always arrived without notice. In time, Macquarie reduced the unit cost per convict to about a quarter of what it had been when he arrived, but this was of little use in the face of naïve political hopes that New South Wales could not only become self-supporting but return a profit. The development costs of the colony, whose boundaries he had been urged to expand, were also resented on the grounds that roads, decent administrative facilities and other amenities could be justified only when the community they served was prepared to pay for them itself. Against this background Macquarie's small indulgences in the way of dignified travel arrangements and well-designed public buildings became easy to condemn as reckless extravagance.

At first, his convict policies were less contentious, in Britain at least. He set himself firmly against abuses of the system, particularly those occurring on the voyage out. Ill-fed and scandalously overcrowded on their transports, with few if any medical facilities, many prisoners died or arrived close to death. Women and girls were preyed on and forced into prostitution by sailors, military escorts and fellow prisoners. Macquarie instituted a system of independent medical supervision on board and would personally inspect shiploads of convicts as they arrived. To the economically minded, fit prisoners, capable of work and able to support themselves were better than sick ones who were a charge on the public purse. Macquarie sought to assign convict servants to responsible masters and female convicts only to married couples, he legislated against unwarranted corporal punishment and did all he could to mitigate violent judicial floggings. He was liberal with free pardons and probationary "tickets of leave" for the skilled, the useful and the well-behaved and he encouraged emancipists – the ex-convicts – into small self-sustaining farming communities. This was intended to· speed up agricultural development and provide them with a living. Once their sentences expired, convicts had either to stay in New South Wales or pay their own fares home.

Macquarie came to believe passionately that convicts could be transformed into good citizens. To him, this was self-evident since so many emancipists had prospered in the colony and a few had become immensely rich. Macquarie was keen to involve these successful men in his administration, finding them easier to work with, more capable and less self-interested than free settlers. Often they had been transported as teenagers for minor acts of civil or military disobedience, but even the great majority of conditioned criminals from city slums had suddenly found their lives transformed in New South Wales. They had access to fresh air and sunshine, nutritious food, free clothing and opportunities to work. Many settled happily to honest lives and had no wish to return to Britain. Their children, born in the colony, were beginning to reach maturity.

In New South Wales, Macquarie's attitudes to convicts and emancipists were unpopular with a small but influential group known as exclusives. They considered themselves an elite and entitled to preferential treatment in the form of big land grants and a ready supply of free convict labour, including the skilled men whom

Macquarie preferred to employ on improving the colony's infrastructure. The exclusives were mainly wealthy free settlers, army officers and churchmen. They often had something shady in their own past to live down, while others had risen from poverty and were self-righteous in their own virtue. As a class, they tended to appreciate the disciplinary value of the brutal floggings which revolted Macquarie.

In one important respect the exclusives were right. It was the large estates that would establish sheep-grazing as the basis of Australia's future prosperity, while small yeomen farmers achieved at best only a personal self-sufficiency. Many failed or illegally sold off their land. Macquarie had seen sheep-grazing dispossess too many small tenant farmers in the Scottish Highlands and considered stock-rearing a lazy option. He also resented the well-born's easy assumption of privilege over those, like himself, who had to make their own way in the world. It was a useful bias. Sheep-grazing established itself without the official indulgence that might have turned the country into a series of huge estates manned by a harshly disciplined convict workforce, reminiscent of slave plantations. Instead, by offering land and opportunity to the majority, Macquarie ensured the development of a broadly based society. In particular, he was determined that those born in New South Wales should have a stake in its future.

young Lachlan

In March 1814, his own son was born in New South Wales. Elizabeth had suffered many miscarriages and young Lachlan nearly died within a few days of birth. His doting parents were inclined to be over-protective and he enjoyed an indulged and privileged life in the colony, though Macquarie did not envisage a future for him there. He was heir to a Mull estate. Instead, at one stage Macquarie cherished the idea that his brother Charles might succeed him as Governor. Other family protégées, the underage lieutenants of 1805, came out to New South Wales as his aides-de-camp but they distinguished themselves only in fast living and became a liability. Macquarie's confidence in Elizabeth had been better placed. She entered fully into his interests and, in some respects, seemed to go further than he did in promoting controversial policies. She particularly identified with Macquarie's insistence on treating emancipists as the social equals of exclusives and inviting them to dine together at Government House, but rather than easing tensions, this exacerbated them. Newly arrived army officers and the advocates sent from England to form a civic judiciary repeatedly sided with those unwilling to meet or work with emancipists on any basis of equality. There were boycotts of Government House hospitality and Macquarie became estranged from his own regiment and the one sent to replace it.

The Father of Australia

Growing friction and obstruction from exclusives and others, whose interests he had crossed, slowly made Macquarie more entrenched in sometimes contradictory views and more authoritarian in his methods. Though objectively he supported the transition to civil law, he found it difficult to adapt to a legal framework that limited his own powers over intransigent officials. He considered their opposition an affront to the Governor's office, his health suffered and his impressive energy became dissipated in quarrels. The exclusives had always had the money and contacts to put their case forcefully in London and, from 1815, their sustained chorus of complaints began to key in with important political developments. Long years of war, culminating in the defeat of Napoleon at Waterloo, had led to severe economic depression and pressure for change. Soon the whole issue of transportation became a useful platform for attacks on Lord Liverpool's government.

Convict numbers were rising alarmingly. Fit young criminals could no longer be pressed into military service, there were no jobs for returning soldiers and widespread general unemployment was causing crime and civil disorder. There was also a scandalised public perception that many criminals welcomed transportation to sunny New South Wales where they enjoyed much better conditions and prospects than the honest poor at home. Free settlers had to pay their own fares and many who might have wished to emigrate could not raise the money.

Once the political bandwagon had started to roll, those opposed to transportation because it was too soft, made common cause with those, like William Wilberforce, the anti-slavery campaigner, who condemned it as inhumane. Others wished to end the system on economic grounds, claiming it cost the country more than poor relief. Distance allowed scope for misrepresentation and Macquarie found himself accused of the very abuses he had campaigned most vigorously against, while the continued existence of hardened criminals in New South Wales was presented as a failure of his enlightened policies.

Capricious judgements against trouble-makers who had challenged his authority also came back to haunt him. In 1816, he punished those preparing a petition to Parliament accusing him of abuse of power. The petition related to his treatment of a clergyman who had made a provocative seizure of a welcome American trading ship, which was technically an enemy vessel, and floggings he had ordered for persistent trespassers in Government House grounds, which had become a resort for petty criminals. The victims, though unsavoury types, turned out to be free men who could not legally be flogged. In 1818, after the customary time-lags, Macquarie was mortified to be censured for blocking the petition when he had counted on Colonial Office support. In Britain, however, the affair had become a cause célébre. Macquarie refused to reinstate a solicitor involved, an action later vindicated when signatures on the petition were found to be forged, and he sent in his own resignation.

The reply, urging him to reconsider, was lost, if not waylaid in transit, but in London events had already moved on. In 1817, Lord Bathurst, the Colonial Secretary, had been forced to propose a Commission of Enquiry into Macquarie's governorship and the perceived failures of transportation. He managed to delay its implementation until 1819 and then Macquarie only learned of it five days before the Commissioner, John Bigge, arrived on his fact-finding mission. Bigge was armed with an impressive array of powers and would spend over a year in the colony. Macquarie welcomed the opportunity to explain his actions, but Bigge was more alert to political realities. He largely ignored Macquarie's views while gathering unsworn evidence from his detractors and countermanding some of his initiatives. Demoralised and marginalized, Macquarie worked on steadily at routine administration for two more years until Lord Brisbane arrived to replace him on a much higher salary, late in 1821. The despised job that had meant obscurity and exile in 1809 had become a prestigious one.

In January 1822, Macquarie set sail for England, leaving behind him a thriving colony with over three times the European population he had found there. Its boundaries had been pushed far beyond the Blue Mountains that had once hemmed in the mainland settlement. Four times as much land was under cultivation and vast new reserves had been opened up. Starvation was no longer a threat.

Stability and a civilised tone had made New South Wales the most attractive of Britain's colonies to free settlers, while a huge increase in convict numbers had been absorbed despite the relaxation of military controls. A civic judiciary had been established after a difficult start, caused largely by the pretensions of early advocates. Restrictions intended to protect Indian trade and British government revenue had to some extent been resolved or circumvented to allow vigorous commercial activity to develop. A makeshift currency of obsolete Spanish silver dollars, overstamped as sterling had been introduced in place of rum and unreliable promissory notes, and a bank was succeeding too well to be closed down by the time the Colonial Office advised against it. A combination of misunderstanding and determined deviousness also secured a badly needed hospital built with funds generated from rum

An Australian bicentenary souvenir inspired by Macquarie's 1813 coinage.

sales, while other civic improvements, on which Macquarie had set his heart, were carried out as a means of employing the convict workforce and paid for out of harbour dues ostensibly raised to finance a police force. Some of these contrivances were bound to attract official disapproval when enquired into too closely. In the short term they would also serve to justify a host of petty grievances and malicious accusations.

Australian black swans which Macquarie sent as presents to landowning friends in Britain and tried to introduce onto Loch Ba, in Mull.

Macquarie's discomfiture and Bigge's identification with the exclusives' concerns had caused their expectations to soar, but it was already too late. Those born in the difficult early years of the colony were now of an age to start influencing its development. Most were of convict parentage or had emancipist leanings and were of limited interest to Bigge, but Macquarie had done much to shape a vision of a new country, which might one day rival America. With this in mind, he proposed in 1817 that the name Australia should replace the old explorers' terminology of New Holland and New South Wales. It derived from the "terra *australis*", the great "*southern* land" that geographers had speculated about since classical times, and as a name it had been in occasional use since at least 1814. As often happened the Colonial Office ignored the suggestion, but in the last, troubled years of his administration, as politicians in London grew heated over a penal colony called New South Wales, Macquarie with his mind on wider horizons, made a point of using "Australia" in official correspondence.

On his departure, life grew harder for transported convicts but attempts to reverse his free pardons and the land grants made to emancipists failed. His guiding principle that convicts had a right to be treated as free men and women once their sentences had expired was eventually properly established and Australia continued to develop broadly in line with his intentions. It was in following years that leaders of the younger generation, whose aspirations he had encouraged, came to look back on Macquarie as the true Father of Australia. By then he was dead, but Elizabeth was grateful for this belated tribute and recorded it on his tombstone.

The Macquaries of Jarvisfield

Macquarie, his wife and son arrived back in England in July 1822. He spent some weeks in London trying to secure the pension promised him by Lord Castlereagh, the long departed Colonial Secretary of 1809. It was not forthcoming and his other intended source of income had also evaporated. In 1816, his brother Charles had acted for him in buying up a new swathe of land along Loch na Keal from the disintegrating estates of the spendthrift sixth Duke of Argyll. At its western end lay Oskamull and his mother's old farmstead. She had died in 1810, aged 82, but his sister's family still farmed there. The purchase used up all his remaining capital and Charles had failed to keep him informed of his tenants' inability to pay their rents after several bad harvests. Macquarie only learned of this when he arrived in Britain to find his bank account empty of the accumulated rents he had relied on.

That autumn in Mull they found Gruline farmhouse uninhabitable and stayed with the hospitable Campbells of nearby Knock, but Elizabeth soon fell ill. To aid her recovery the family took a leisured tour on the continent as they had once hoped to do early in the marriage. Their return to London in July 1823 coincided with the publication of the Bigge report. It was an apparently well-reasoned document recommending the progression of New South Wales, by degrees, to full colonial status, but Macquarie was presented as an impediment to such progress. The report received wide coverage, including a damaging personal attack on Macquarie in the *Edinburgh Review*, but his attempts to rebut false claims and explain his administration continued to meet with scant attention. He retreated again to Mull, deeply demoralised and increasingly hard up.

The patched and repatched Gruline house was seldom watertight and the family stayed first at Knock then lodged uncomfortably in their own home while Macquarie paced out the plan of the mansion that he still hoped to build and busied himself with the life of a Highland laird. This consisted mainly of long rides in foul weather to sit as a magistrate at his model village of Salen. Despite the hardships, he claimed that these quiet months with Elizabeth in their own home were happy ones, but as the wet spring progressed she grew uneasy to see him setting his affairs in order. He now spoke of the estate as belonging to their son and he made an extended round of farewells.

In April 1824, he returned to London intent on salvaging his reputation and making provision for his family, if need be by finding a new military command. Already, politics had moved on, while among those still interested in New South Wales, Bigge's motives, including recommendations that benefited his own family were coming under scrutiny. The difficulty over the withheld pension, partly a matter of lost paperwork, was suddenly easy to resolve and Macquarie found himself welcome

*A fashionable silhouette of
Lachlan Macquarie, Junior*

*Macquarie Mausoleum,
Gruline*

Detail of Calachally and Salen

Lachlan Macquarie's Jarvisfield estate is now only recalled in Salen street names.

again in London society where he had been cold-shouldered only a short while before. He selected a school for his son and continued to work for the interests of those seeking his help, whether in Britain or Australia. Ignoring frequent bouts of ill-health, he embarked on an energetic social life reminiscent of his happy days as Assistant Adjutant-General twenty years earlier, but now it was a means of saying good-bye. In May he was told by Bathurst that he could not be considered for the title that he still half hoped for, though he was cheered by an audience with King George IV. Two days later, on 11th June, he entered his final illness.

Elizabeth and young Lachlan hurried south to be with him and arrived six days before his death on 1st July. Among those present in his long funeral cortege as it crossed London, were the Duke of Argyll and the Earl of Breadalbane, while the Duke of Wellington, Lord Bathurst and many others sent their carriages as a mark of respect. His body was taken to Mull for burial in a spot he had chosen and his baby daughter, Jane Jarvis Macquarie, who had died in Perth in 1808, was disinterred to be buried with him.

Elizabeth coped with grief and guilt that she had remained silent over Macquarie's awareness of his approaching death, by reading through his journals and the vast correspondence he had kept since he first set out for India. She soon came to idealise his memory. That autumn, she moved to the outskirts of London to be near her son's school, staying in cheap lodgings, which distressed her friends. Macquarie's pension had died with him, but the sale of his major-general's commission had brought her a little, much needed capital. Charles Forbes, the Bombay financier, now a British M.P. managed to secure her a widow's pension, but she embarrassed him and a fellow sponsor by holding out for her husband's reputation. She insisted that Macquarie's answers to the findings of the Bigge Commission must first be published. This was refused, but other influences were independently at work, fighting for emancipists' rights in New South Wales. In 1828, Sir James Mackintosh, the former judge in Bombay, and now an influential M.P. managed to force partial publication of Macquarie's two papers. Elizabeth then felt able to accept her pension and a friend's bequest further eased her finances. She would remain careful with money, though generous to those in need.

Young Lachlan appeared unaffected by the family's reversals of fortune. He settled happily to school in Temple Grove in Surrey where he was popular, though inclined to command and disinclined to study. His close friendship with William Drummond, eldest son of his godfather and guardian, Sir James Drummond, now Viscount Strathallan of Strathallan Castle in Perthshire, seemed advantageous. He and his mother stayed regularly at the Castle as they travelled between London and Mull each summer. It soon became a second home to Lachlan, who did not share his mother's frugal tastes and began to find her protective care stifling. In 1831, at the age of 16, he joined the army against her better judgement. He was already showing signs of frenzied excitement and instability which increased with the customary excesses of military life.

In 1830, Elizabeth moved north to Aberdeen and the next year returned to live permanently at Gruline. She could now afford to mark her husband's grave with a handsome tombstone, commemorating at length achievements that it had not suited the government to honour. The rigours of the Gruline winters once again affected her health, she suffered repeated colds and died there in March 1835, aged 56.

In the following year, Lachlan married Isabella Campbell, third daughter of a landowner on the island of Jura, but her dowry was very much smaller than he had anticipated. He also grew impatient of army life, having passed through the usual stages of purchased commissions in a variety of regiments. In 1841, he sold his captaincy in the Scots Greys and retired to live on the Jarvisfield estate, which he had enlarged with the purchase of Glenforsa after his uncle Charles' death. In apparent rejection of the memory of his father's first wife, Jane Jarvis, he used the name Glenforsa for the entire property, but a letter of 1823 hints that his father may have intended to make the change.

In Mull, Lachlan's eccentric behaviour and growing debauchery were tolerated at first, but he handed down wilfully archaic sentences as a magistrate at Salen and on occasion his unfortunate wife was forced to abandon Gruline. An extravagant life-style put him heavily in debt to William Drummond and, in 1844, he altered his will in his favour and made him a trustee. A few months later, in May 1845, he died as a result of a fall on the stairs of Craignish Castle, his wife's family home. The fall followed a drunken carouse with Drummond. He was only 31 and had no children. His widow, Isabella, inherited the Gruline house and some contents under the altered will but in time, she relinquished both the house and remaining Macquarie mementoes to the Greenhill-Gardynes the family of William Drummond's son-in-law, in exchange for an annuity. It was an amicable arrangement. The Greenhill-Gardynes were among several incoming families, free of old squabbles and old debts who would make a positive contribution to Mull and gain the affection of local people.

Young Lachlan's travelling medicine chest.

The Last MacQuarries of Ulva

The last chief of the MacQuarries, the 16th in line, was another Lachlan MacQuarrie, customarily known as Ulva, since landowners used the names of their principal property as a form of courtesy title. The clan's territory was meagre, centering on Ulva and including some much smaller islands to the south. Staffa was a distant outlier to the south-west and a little land round Lagganulva provided a foothold on mainland Mull. All this seldom supported more than 50-60 fighting men and their families, forcing the MacQuarries to ally themselves with stronger neighbouring clans, but they went to war wearing their own red and green tartan (see back cover) and spurred on by their own battle-cry "An t-arm breac dearg" (The red tartan army).

The Macleans of Duart, dominant on Mull at the time, took the MacQuarries into the Civil War on the side of Charles I and the clan never recovered from a defeat at Inverkeithing in 1651. There, Hector Maclean of Duart made a reckless last stand, sacrificing hundreds of followers he could have led to safety, and leaving Mull weakened and vulnerable. Equally unworldly were notions of independence from the Scottish crown, which led the MacQuarries and neighbouring chiefs to neglect payments due to feudal overlords. This burdened their descendants with huge debts and legal expenses once evasion was no longer possible.

The last chief was born to this difficult inheritance in about 1715 and succeeded his father in 1735. In 1745, the powerful Duke of Argyll kept him and other local chiefs out of the second, disastrous Jacobite rebellion, but he was particularly vulnerable to the pressures that bankrupted many Highland chiefs in the years that followed. The transition from payment in kind and barter to a cash economy put too many temptations in the way of the those used to much plainer living. Ulva's weakness for Lowland luxuries, combined with the expansive traditions of Highland hospitality and a poor grasp of estate management did nothing to liquidate old debts and added many new ones.

His personal life was equally untidy. He was said to have tricked his first wife Alice into marriage by forging a letter of rejection from her intended husband. She was a noted Gaelic poet and sister of the influential Allan Maclean of Torloisk, who was active in raising Highland regiments. Alice and Ulva had eight children before she died in 1755, then he had several more by her maid whom he was pressured into marrying by the local minister in 1767.

In 1777, creditors forced the sale of Ulva's whole estate and that of a junior branch of the family at Ormaig. Ownership of ancestral lands was more important than strict primogeniture in determining Highland chieftainship and the MacQuarries were left leaderless. Although he was over 60 a living of sorts was found for the former chief as a lieutenant in a Highland regiment sent out to fight in the American

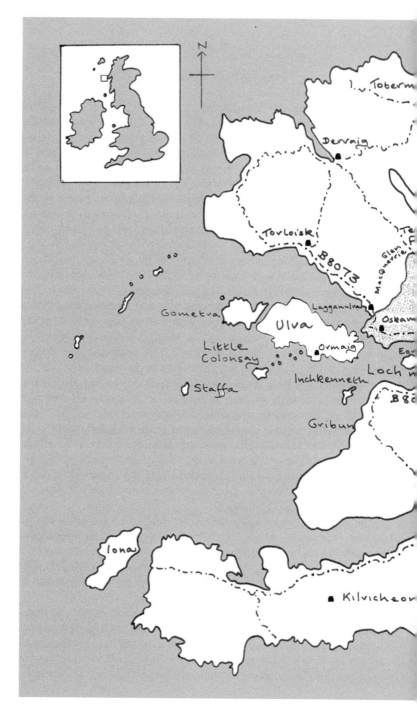

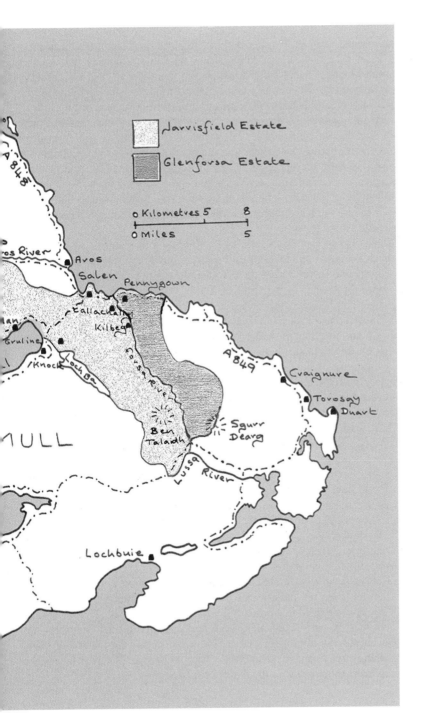

Jarvisfield Estate

Glenforsa Estate

0 Kilometres 5   8
0 Miles   5

Aros River
Aros
Salen
Pennygown
Tallachain
Kilbeg
Gruline
Knock
Loch Ba
Forsa River
A 849
Craignure
Torosay
Duart
Sgurr
Dearg
Ben
Talaidh
MULL
Lussa River
Lochbuie

War of Independence in 1778. He returned in 1782 and lived on in fretful poverty for over 30 years as a subsistence farmer, first on Little Colonsay and then at Gribun. Lachlan Macquarie and Allan Maclean did their best to help his children, and Murdoch Maclaine of Lochbuie, a cousin on his mother's side, managed some residual money and guaranteed the old man's rent to prevent seizure of his cattle.

Ulva, the island, meanwhile prospered after 1785 under a business-like new owner, Colin Macdonald of Boisdale. His father had introduced and refined an Irish technique of rendering down kelp and other seaweeds to produce alkali-rich ash, also known as kelp, on his home island of South Uist in 1730. The practice became widespread, reaching Mull during the old chief's tenure but he had ignored this valuable source of income. The alkali was vital to Britain's soap and glass-making industries and the bleaching trade when war disrupted foreign imports, and huge profits could be made.

Macdonald and his son Ranald lived in style, building a mansion, Ulva House, to replace old MacQuarrie's cottage home and entertaining rich and well-born tourists deprived of continental travel during the Napoleonic wars. A fashionable new destination had been discovered in the form of Staffa, whose soaring basalt columns and echoing caves had been recently revealed to a wider world by the distinguished scientist, Sir Joseph Banks. Ranald Macdonald styled himself Staffa, after the more famous island, and transformed Ulva into a visitor attraction for his guests. There were pipers to serenade them, colourful boats to row them to Staffa and prosperous, well-housed tenants to provide a romanticized view of Highland life. All this collapsed with the end of the war and the kelp profits it had generated. By 1817, Ranald Macdonald's estate looked likely to come on the market.

It may have been some comfort to the old chief just before he died in 1818 to realize that Macquaries might soon regain Ulva. He had long watched with satisfaction the rise of Lachlan Macquarie and his brother Charles, and he had been happy to allow Lachlan use of his coat of arms, a procedure which neither may have realized was incorrect. Charles Macquarie, still troubled by the head wound sustained in Egypt, had retired from the army as a lieutenant colonel in 1811. The following year he married the much younger Marianne Willison. She was the daughter of a successful portrait painter enriched by the Indian fortune of a man whose life he had once saved. Marianne's money was firmly settled on herself and her children, but may have given Charles a false sense of prosperity. He was also inclined to overestimate his brother's wealth.

Having had his eye on Ulva in 1818, Charles invested unwisely in land round Duart in 1821, then tried the patience of the financially embarrassed Lachlan by requesting loans and suggesting he take Glenforsa off his hands. Charles finally purchased Ulva in 1825 after Lachlan's death and managed to sell Duart but not Glenforsa. He moved his family into Ulva House but three years later Marianne died, compounding his financial difficulties. The children of the marriage were still minors and their money was in the hands of trustees.

For ten years, up to his own death in 1835, Charles could call himself Macquarie of Ulva in the style of the old MacQuarrie chiefs, but an overt claim to the chieftainship was blocked. John MacQuarrie of Ballygartan, a closer cousin of the last chief, had a tenuous but unexercised claim to some residual land rights, which he was not prepared to relinquish, even for the large sum of money Charles reputedly offered him. When Ulva was sold in 1836 to settle Charles' debts, an improbable new claimant to the chieftainship came forward. This was his nephew, young Lachlan Macquarie of Jarvisfield, whose estate included what had once been ancestral MacQuarrie land round Kellan Mill on Loch na Keal but no-one took these pretensions seriously and there were no heirs in a position to press them further.

Macquarie's Mull

Salen – Macquarie's model village

History: Salen lies at the southern end of the A848 on Mull's east coast. It marks the eastern corner of Macquarie's Jarvisfield estate and may have been chosen for its good anchorage facing the Scottish mainland. Before 1808, decrepit crofts and a ruinous church skirted the Great Moss of Salen, a wide stretch of bogland, which Macquarie had ditched and drained. He gave instructions for sixteen crofters' homes to be built and specified square-cornered, gabled cottages with proper chimneys, mortared masonry and two glazed windows.

Model villages were fashionable improvements for those wishing to regenerate and modernise the Highlands. They were characterised by solidly built houses, concentrations of skilled tradesmen and amenities unfamiliar to the traditional groupings of farmhouses known as townships. The third Duke of Argyll founded Scotland's first planned town close to his famous new castle at Inveraray in 1744 and in 1804, Macquarie toured this estate as a guest of the fifth Duke, another keen improver. On Mull, Tobermory was built as a planned town by the British Fisheries Association in 1788 and local landowners who wished to seem modern, were planning model villages of their own by 1799.

As was customary, new occupants at Salen built their own houses, but received some financial support and rent rebates for three years. The skilled craftsmen specified were a blacksmith, joiner, carpenter, shoemaker, tailor and woodsman. Macquarie also helped a schoolteacher, Archibald Macquarie, gain better qualifications and an inn was established. A shop, inappropriately set up in the church session house while he was abroad, and forced to relocate by indignant parishioners, served Mull well during the 1846-8 potato famine.

On occasion, expenses such as carting manure to improve the croft of widowed Flora Macquarie, were met under Macquarie's orders from New South Wales. Fertile fields enabled crofters to pay their rents more regularly, and rents were intended to be a large part of Macquarie's retirement income.

From 1816, Macquarie's plans for Salen started to take on characteristics of plans realised or thwarted in New South Wales. He envisaged a distillery, water-mill and post-office and a change of name to Port Macquarie. Salen kept its name, perhaps because the Australian Port Macquarie became a forced labour camp for recalcitrant convicts and persistent escapers in 1821, but from the 1860s, when the pier was built, Salen became Mull's principal cattle exporting port. Nor did Macquarie live long enough to proceed with a distillery or other projects but he regularly rode three miles each way in the unpleasant winter of 1823-4 to sit as a magistrate at Salen. In the last weeks of his life, while in London, he negotiated successfully with the Commissioners for Building Additional Places of Worship in the Highlands and Islands of Scotland to include Salen in their programme of new or improved churches and manses for ministers to live in. This established it as the centre of a reconstituted parish replacing Torosay and the ruinous church of Penny-gown.

Buildings: Rock Cottage is on the corner of Salen's original curved main street where it joins the present A849 at the south-east end of the village. The cottage was built in about 1820, during Macquarie's life-time. The two chimneys, one in each gable, indicate its original size and they and the glazed windows on either side of the

Rock Cottage

front door are typical of most improved cottages in the area. This croft's arable fields lay directly across the road.

Most of Macquarie's other cottages lined the northern side of the old main street, closer to the modern Gruline road junction. This is very unlike the random scatter of old township houses that can be seen at Ormaig on Ulva (p.36). The Lounge Bar window of the present Salen Hotel, looks out over crofters' fields which ran down to the sea. The hotel car park, across the road, overlooks the shrunken Great Moss, which was drained to provide grazing land. Dark sedge indicates the remaining marshland, while upcast from the principal drainage channels created walkways across it. One of these became a new route to Gruline, the start of the present B8035.

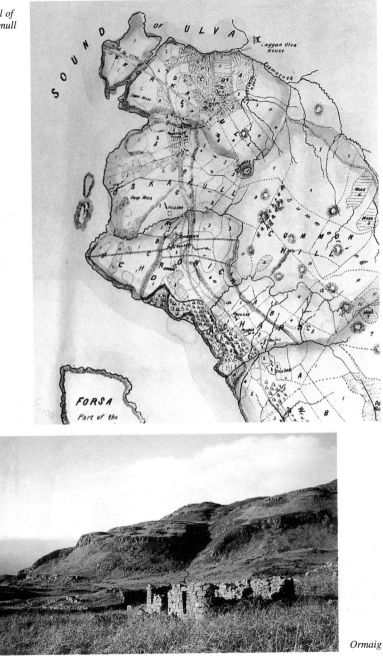

Detail of
Oskamull

Ormaig

Burial Ground, Kilvickewen

Ulva Church

The church of 1899 has replaced the one built in 1827 at Macquarie's instigation, but the manse survives, though much altered. It can be seen well, though from a slight distance, by taking the first right turn off the Gruline road into Jarvisfield Road and right again into Jarvisfield Place. Beyond is the glebe land where the minister could graze his cow, with the Manse at the far end.

It was built to a standard design by Thomas Telford, Scotland's great engineer and road builder of the period. The two-storey main block had three windows at each level and was flanked by two small porches for the front and back doors, an arrangement that survives little changed on a former manse of identical design at Tobermory (now known as Mansefield, in Breadalbane Street). Church, manse, glebe and stipend for a minister had been statutory requirements in Mull's historic parishes since 1609, but most local landlords shirked these responsibilities.

The Jarvisfield street names date from the 1970s and are the only survival on Mull of the name Macquarie chose for his estate in memory of his first wife, Jane Jarvis, who did not live to share it with him.

Macquarie's inn still stands on the north side of the road to Tobermory, just before the bridge. It is a two storey house that opens in summer as The Coffee Pot tearoom.

Salen Manse today

Gruline

The Mausoleum, is three miles from Salen off the B8035 road. It is signed a quarter of a mile beyond the turning to Ulva Ferry and reached via the drive to Gruline Farm. A gate beyond gives access to the mausoleum where cars can park. Macquarie chose this site in April 1824, when he felt death approaching and was buried here on 29 July 1824. In 1832, his widow placed a flat stone of finely carved red granite over the grave and it was later set upright in the south-eastern doorway of the Victorian mausoleum. The Rev. David Bell from Fife helped Elizabeth Macquarie to compose the inscription. Above is the Macquarie coat of arms, properly belonging to the last clan chief who allowed its use by Macquarie as a distinguished member of the fading clan. The text on the stone reads:

HERE, IN THE HOPE OF A GLORIOUS RESURRECTION
LIE THE REMAINS OF THE LATE
MAJOR GENERAL LACHLAN MACQUARIE
OF JARVISFIELD
WHO WAS BORN 31ST JANUARY, 1761
AND DIED AT LONDON, ON THE 1ST OF JULY, 1824.
THE PRIVATE VIRTUES AND AMIABLE DISPOSITION
WITH WHICH HE WAS ENDOWED
RENDERED HIM AT ONCE A MOST BELOVED HUSBAND,
FATHER AND MASTER AND A MOST ENDEARING FRIEND.
HE ENTERED THE ARMY AT THE AGE OF FIFTEEN,
AND THROUGHOUT THE PERIOD OF 47 YEARS,
SPENT IN THE PUBLIC SERVICE,
WAS UNIFORMLY CHARACTERIZED
BY ANIMATED ZEAL FOR HIS PROFESSION, ACTIVE BENEVOLENCE
AND GENEROSITY WHICH KNEW NO BOUNDS.
HE WAS APPOINTED GOVERNOR OF NEW SOUTH WALES A.D. 1809
AND FOR TWELVE YEARS FULFILLED THE DUTIES OF THAT STATION
WITH EMINENT ABILITY AND SUCCESS.
HIS SERVICES IN THAT CAPACITY
HAVE JUSTLY ATTACHED A LASTING HONOUR TO HIS NAME.
THE WISDOM, LIBERALITY AND BENEVOLENCE
OF ALL THE MEASURES OF HIS ADMINISTRATION
HIS RESPECT FOR THE ORDINANCES OF RELIGION
AND THE READY ASSISTANCE WHICH HE GAVE
TO EVERY CHARITABLE INSTITUTION
THE UNWEARIED ASSIDUITY WITH WHICH HE SOUGHT TO PROMOTE
THE WELFARE OF ALL CLASSES OF THE COMMUNITY
THE RAPID IMPROVEMENT OF THE COLONY UNDER HIS AUSPICES
AND THE HIGH ESTIMATION IN WHICH BOTH HIS CHARACTER
AND GOVERNMENT WERE HELD
RENDERED HIM TRULY DESERVING OF THE APPELLATION
BY WHICH HE HAS BEEN DISTINGUISHED
"THE FATHER OF AUSTRALIA."

The white marble panel in the north-west doorway commemorates Macquarie, his second wife and children as follows:

WITHIN THIS VAULT REST THE MORTAL REMAINS
OF THE LATE
MAJOR GENERAL MACQUARIE OF JARVISFIELD,
WHO DIED IN LONDON, ON THE 1ST JULY 1824.
HIS WIFE
ELISABETH HENRIETTA CAMPBELL, WHO DIED
AT JARVISFIELD, ON THE 17TH OF MARCH 1835. THEIR DAUGHTER
JANE JARVIS, WHO DIED IN PERTH, ON THE
5TH DECEMBER 1808, AGED 3 MONTHS
AND THEIR SON
LACHLAN, WHO DIED AT CRAIGNISH CASTLE
ON THE 7TH OF MAY 1845, AGED 32.

"I KNOW THAT MY REDEEMER LIVETH, AND THAT HE SHALL
STAND AT THE LATTER DAY UPON THE EARTH."
JOB XIX XXV

With its buttressed walls of dressed sandstone, elegantly shaped doorways and decorative finials, the mausoleum has the air of a miniature chapel. It was probably planned by Macquarie on the lines of a plainer mausoleum built in 1777 by the 17th chief of the Maclaines of Lochbuie, his mother's family, but it remained un-built at the time of his son's death in 1845. It is now maintained by the National Trust of Australia. Possibly it was put up as a gesture by the Drummond family, who successfully fought off a challenge to young Lachlan's will by a Macquarie cousin in 1851. The circular enclosure is reminiscent of early Celtic Christian burial grounds more common in Ireland than in Scotland.

Loch Ba and Old Gruline House

Half a mile south of the turning to the Mausoleum where the B8035 loops tightly round Knock house, a track leads to Loch Ba. Cars can park beside the gate.

The track follows the west shore of the loch and gives excellent views of the south-west side of Jarvisfield culminating in the tall conical peak of Ben Talaidh. From a boat on the loch, on his son's tenth birthday, Macquarie pointed out to his family their inheritance, to the dismay of Elizabeth who recognised that he did not

Old Gruline House

expect to live. The hillside high above the nearer end of Loch Ba gives a distant view of Old Gruline House, standing beside the large turreted Victorian mansion, Gruline House. Neither can be visited.

Old Gruline House was built in the late 18th century as a compact modern home for the factor of the Lochbuie estate. There was one ground-floor room besides the kitchen and five very small upstairs rooms below a gabled roof. Macquarie always intended to demolish it and build a mansion on the site. By 1816 he was even considering a small castle, better suited to the fine scenery of Loch Ba, but then he overreached himself financially with a new land purchase. On return to Britain, with his pension in doubt he was prepared to settle for a cottage then realised that even this was beyond his means.

Although his brother Charles' family used Old Gruline House from 1815, Macquarie considered it uninhabitable in 1822 and his family stayed as guests at Knock. Repeated attempts at renovation had made it more or less watertight by 1824, but draughts blew out candles and fires, condensation ran down the walls and Macquarie had no study in which to attend to his paperwork. He wanted no more money spent on the house, which he still hoped to replace, but Elizabeth covertly added a small block of three extra rooms and a porch when he was in London, where he died. His coffin rested briefly in the new extension before his burial.

Elizabeth and young Lachlan continued to use the house on summer visits to Mull and each lived in it more permanently for a few years before their own deaths in 1835 and 1845. Elizabeth failed to get the costs of a new mansion allowed under Macquarie's will, when trustees controlled the estate on her son's behalf and the present Gruline House was built by Lieutenant-Colonel Greenhill-Gardyne, William Drummond's son-in-law. Old Gruline House became an outbuilding and was in poor repair when panelling and doorways from the parlour, probably installed by Elizabeth in 1824, were removed to Macquarie University in Sydney, New South Wales in 1967.

Ulva, Ormaig, Kilvickewen and related sites

Preparation: Ulva welcomes visitors on foot or on mountain bikes but the ferry is too small for cars. The island's many tracks are well signposted to indicate how long an average walker will take to cover the distance and a booklet with route maps is available. The one-room museum, Sheila's Cottage and a tearoom, open from April to mid-October are within very easy walking distance of the ferry. Ulva Church and Bracadale Steadings are within a one mile radius, along rough tracks. A visit to Ormaig and Kilvickewen on the island's magnificent southern coast requires serious walking. Waterproof boots and clothing, picnic food and hot drinks are recommended, especially out of season. In winter and spring, when the bracken is low, the sites are easier to see. Binoculars are useful as well as the Ordnance Survey Pathfinder 328 map of Ulva or Explorer 374. For those who like to linger, picnic and look about them, two separate day visits are strongly advised for the near and further sites, especially when the days are short. Mountain bikes help shorten journey times and although they cannot cope with the final descent to Kilvickewen, they can safely be left beside the path.

Access: Ulva Ferry is signposted off the B8073 road from Gruline. There is parking close to the ferry. From about 1st April to 15th October, the open ferry for foot passengers and cyclists leaves on the hour from 9.00-12.00 and 14.00-17.00. Local Tourist Information Centres will

Improved Cottage

33

have up-to-date information. Out of season, telephone 01688 500 226 or 264 a day or so before a proposed visit. On arrival look for a sliding wooden panel on the wall of the building nearest the slipway and follow the instructions given.

Kelp. At low water, note all the brown seaweeds that brought prosperity to Ulva, from 1785 to 1817 during the kelp boom (see p.26). They were harvested, dried and burnt in shallow, scooped kilns all around the shore from spring to autumn. The William Daniell print on p.43 shows the billowing smoke they generated.

The Museum above the Boathouse tearoom gives an introduction to Ulva past and present.

Sheila's Cottage overlooks the ferry and is named after Sheila MacFadyen, a dairy-maid from Ulva House who lived in the lower end from 1900. The slightly taller of these two joined cottages is an improved house of the

Traditional Cottage

type Macquarie specified for Salen. Its far wall has the characteristic squared corners, raised gable and stone chimney all strengthened with mortar. The two glazed windows at the front of the building are typical.

The lower cottage preserves some traditional features especially the curved outer corners and slanting "hipped" side roof. Stones weigh down the thatch that would probably have been of heather. Inside, the roof-frame is built of rough, wooden poles and the floor is natural rock with pockets of earth. The upper part of the wall that separates the two cottages is made of hurdles.

Keep the features of both cottages in mind for a visit to Ormaig.

Landmarks to Ormaig (a 1½ hour walk). Passing Sheila's Cottage, take the route to South Side at the first and second signposts. Bear left at the third signpost which says only "Farm Circuit" and follow two further signposts indicating South Side and Ormaig. Some distance after the track emerges from mossy woodland and winds round a series of hairpin bends, look down from the second bend to see a neolithic standing stone some way below on a grassy slope. Such stones were set up about 3500 years ago by Britain's first farming communities.

The small roofless building just ahead round the sharp bend is a curious focal point on which all the walls on the centre of the island seem to converge (best seen on the Ordnance Survey Pathfinder 328, 1:25000 map) or Explorer 374. The sheep walk established by the Macdonalds after 1785 stretches across the island's hills to the right. Landlords seeking to make their failing estates more viable were starting

to run their own sheep on land previously rented to tenants for summer grazing.
As the track winds on across the saddle of Ulva, a beautiful scatter of islands off the
southern shore comes into view (see p. 41). On the horizon to the left, the long, low

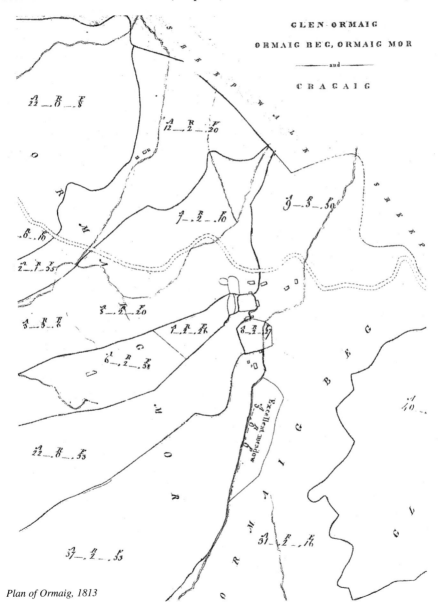

Plan of Ormaig, 1813

silhouette of the Ross of Mull leads the eye directly to Iona at its western end. In the foreground, the largest island with a flat topped central hill is Little Colonsay. Here, the last chief of the MacQuarries farmed disconsolately after losing Ulva. Further out, slightly to the right of Little Colonsay, lies Staffa, looking almost like two islands from this viewpoint.

Ormaig. The cottages of Ormaig are widely dispersed among eight very small farms that fan out across the slope to the sea but a central cluster of buildings stands close to the path. Here a modern cairn has been set up by the Clan MacQuarrie Association. Macquarie is assumed to have a family connection with Ormaig because his younger brother, Charles, born in Lagganulva on Mull in 1771, was brought to Ormaig to be baptised. Baptisms were traditionally carried out in the family home. The stone houses and boundary walls appear to date to the time of Ranald Macdonald since they relate fairly well to an estate map of 1813. Once he had cleared away unsightly homes and improvident tenants, he liked to present Ulva to his many visitors as an ideal Highland community. Skilled workers may have been brought in to build the three improved houses with chimneys in their gables since extensions have been added later using traditional dry stone walling methods.

The homes of Macquarie's boyhood were probably built of turf in a form similar to the round-cornered stone cottages. Slender roofing poles which perched directly on the walls supported turf and heather thatch. This was lashed down with heather ropes weighted with stones that dangled along the eaves. There was minimal furniture, merely low stone or plank benches and crib beds of heather packed with the roots downwards. Cooking was done in a single iron pot, hanging from the roof over a smoky peat fire in the centre of one room. Wood was scarce and doors were often of hurdles. Occasional holes in wall or roof served as windows and were closed with makeshift shutters.

Turf houses were warmer than stone ones and required less effort to build, but turf stripping was ruinous to the grazing land on which these subsistence farmers depended. Their main asset was beef cattle, which were sent south to be fattened up and sold, but they refused to grow fodder crops such as kale, hay or turnips for winter feed. Stunted sheep and cattle had to survive on impoverished turf and field stubble. In prolonged frost or snow, essential animals were kept alive – just – on people's oatmeal. The grazing was also shared by little ponies that were used to carry loads, because of a lack of roads and wheeled vehicles. Before losing his estate, the chief of the MacQuarries rode a brown pony but Lachlan Macquarie does not seem to have ridden as a child. Throughout his career, he needed a quiet, steady horse. Scrawny chickens foraged for themselves but roosted in the houses. Firearms were banned after the 1745 rebellion and foxes were proliferating unchecked.

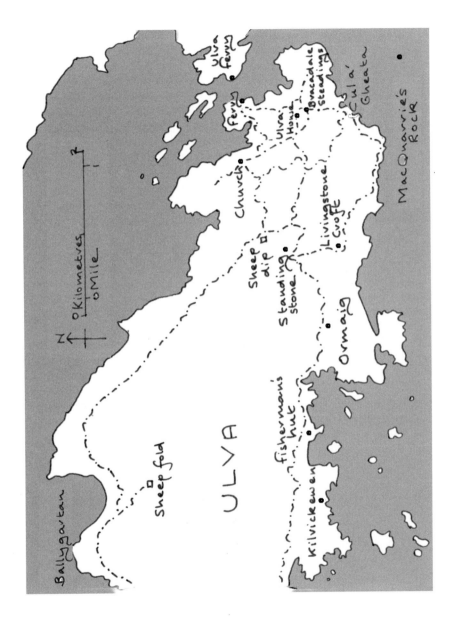

ULVA

Ballygartan

Sheep fold

Kilvickewen

Fisherman's hut

Ormaig

Standing stone

Sheep dip

Church

Livingstone Cave

Ferry

Ulva House

Bracadale steadings

Ula' Gheata

MacQuarrie's Rock

Ulva Ferry

N

0 Kilometres
0 Mile

The staple crops were oats and barley but, by Macquarie's day these were being neglected in favour of cattle rearing and much oatmeal was imported. Old, unenclosed fields marked by cultivation ridges, which deepened the soil and created drainage on boggy slopes, can be widely seen on Mull and Ulva. At Ormaig a flat strip of sedge-infested grassland south of the main settlement is identified on the 1813 plan as an "excellent meadow" but hill pastures were traditionally used for summer grazing. Potatoes, introduced to the region against fierce opposition had proved their worth in tiding families over when wet summers destroyed the grain. They reached Mull in about 1752 and led to further neglect of cereal crops, but made it possible to keep pigs.

Among ordinary people, there was a strong prejudice against growing vegetables although carrots and onions were bought and eaten raw at seasonal fairs. Instead, wild food like cress was appreciated and its habitat noted in placenames. In contrast, the gentry grew a very wide range of vegetables, ordering seeds and plants from Macquarie's uncle Murdoch Maclaine when he was a merchant in Edinburgh.

The generally low standards of cultivation, stock rearing, hygiene and house maintenance were noted with unease by travellers and despaired of by landowners hoping to improve their estates. The best escape route for those who felt trapped in this environment was education and later in life Macquarie would stress the need for the boys he helped to have sufficient schooling to pass for gentlemen. For those who could not afford to become army officers, other professions such as commerce, doctoring or the law could sometimes be learned on the job among networks of relatives, often in Edinburgh, who created opportunities for each other. For the rest, recurrent cycles of bankruptcy for landlords, starvation for tenants and their dependants and dispossession for those the land could not sustain would continue for almost a century.

Kilvickewen

Landmarks and descent to Kilvickewen. As the track curves south-westwards out of Ormaig, the pale gable end of a lobster fisherman's hut can be seen one mile ahead. This is the half-way mark. Half a mile beyond it, a rock wall sweeps down the furthest visible hillside and Kilvickewen lies on the coastal plain below. Just before the track reaches and swings round this high, natural cliff, a roofless cottage with gable and chimney appears downhill on the left. The burial ground is visible, half a mile across the heather, in a dip closer to the sea. It appears as a dark hedge of thornscrub with a small off-white cross to the left. There is no obvious path down and the ground is uneven and boggy. On reaching the top of a small cliff a short distance below the ruined houses, look down onto a boundary wall running towards the cemetery. From a position above this wall, turn right to take an easy, diagonal route down the cliff. The boundary wall offers a relatively dry pathway across the bogland.

Kilvickewen. The Gaelic *Cill mhic Eoghainn* means the church of the son of Eoghan and is thought indicate the site of a very early church founded by Ernan, son of Eoghan. Ernan was St Columba's nephew and fellow-worker at the Iona mission in the 6th century. Kilvickeon, in south Mull has the same dedication and reflects the active church building of these Irish monks. The private burial enclosure of Hector McQuarie of Soriby appears to rest on the foundations of the church, which was apparently ruinous in 1773.

The scatter of anonymous grave markers, often more like rocks than monuments, is characteristic of these ancient cemeteries. Gaelic was an oral culture and family memories were strong. The few inscribed stones preserve local names: Livingstones, MacLaines, McKinnons, McArthurs, McDonalds, McNeils and especially Macquaries. The earliest commemorates John McGuarie (Macquarie) of Balligarten who put up and dated his own stone in 1765, but did not die until 1773.

The private burial enclosure to the west was built by Charles Macquarie for his family and probably marks the spot where his mother, father, brother Donald and two infant brothers are buried. Lachlan Macquarie paid one pound for a stone to mark his father's grave in 1785, but this does not survive. Charles' stone, assuming his family could afford one, has also disappeared, while his wife's white marble tablet has become detached from the wall and its inscription is fading. It reads "Sacred to the memory of • MARIANN WILLISON • spouse of • Charles Macquarie of Ulva • Lieut Colonel 42nd Regt • She lived beloved & respected • the friend to the friendless • the affectionate domestic mother • and • the wife according to the husband's heart • died 3rd Sept 1828 • aged 36 years." Although it was customary for women to keep their father's name after marriage, as a gentleman's wife, Marianne would normally have been referred to as Mrs Macquarie. Prominent on the wall is a tablet to her second son, Captain George Willison Macquarie who died at Salen in 1894.

Ulva House in 1813

Return to the North Side. To return to the track, follow the boundary wall across the waterlogged ground to the cliff, walk left along the base of the cliff and take the easy diagonal route up it, passing above a conspicuous green clump of ivy on the rock face. From the ruined cottages, paths of sorts lead back onto the main track. Do not be tempted to follow the track westwards in a circuit of the island, since it peters out in rockfalls. It is necessary to return via Ormaig. Once across the island's saddle, other routes to the ferry are indicated and times given.

The Livingstone Croft and alternative Macquarie birthplaces. Various 1930s traditions which seem to confuse Macquarie's birthplace with those of other local figures focus on sites close to Ormaig. Two of them are reached by a pleasant detour way-marked with white-topped posts, which leads to the ferry after about one and a half hour's walking. The path starts just above the roofless hut where the walls converge (see p.34) and runs southwards in a narrow gap between a stone wall and a wire fence.

After three quarters of a mile, the Livingstone Croft can be identified by a freestanding white notice board now devoid of text. It stands on the western side of a scattered settlement of ruined houses. The croft, in the strict sense, was a small farm which was rented by the grandparents of the famous missionary explorer Dr David Livingstone and his father was born in the cottage attached to it. In 1792, the family left Ulva to make a better living in the textile mills of Blantyre near Glasgow, but the position of the croft is known because Dr Livingstone came back to find it in 1864.

Macquarie's origins seem to have become entwined with this story. Hearsay recorded in 1938 describes his father as a fisherman crofter who "lived almost next door to... Livingstone's father's house." Ormaig, with which Macquarie's father did have some connection, is the next door village, half a mile to the west as the crow flies, but the crofter-fisherman was probably Livingstone's grandfather. After 1785, the Macdonalds encouraged fishing by helping tenants acquire the heavy boats needed for herring nets. Macquarie's father died in 1775 and family records describe him as a house carpenter and miller.

40

About a mile eastwards along the path is Cul a gheata, a rocky promontory on the shore, where a track leads inland to the Bracadale Steadings directly to the north. In a story recorded in 1939 General Macquarie is supposed to have led his guest "a big Englishman" to agree that little could be expected from someone born in one of "the little houses or huts" he indicates at Cul a gheata, then he reveals this to be his own birthplace. An account published in 1797 by the French naturalist Faujas de Saint Fond concerns General Allan Maclean of Torloisk's brother who took pride in showing his guest the hut where they were born. Over time, the story appears to have become attached to the wrong general while the guest, a noted Frenchman, has evolved into a big Englishman. The relevance to Cul a gheata, where there is no evidence of houses, is not clear, but the name translates to "Back of the Gate." It is just possible that some euphemism for illegitimacy has been misunderstood over the generations as stories switched between English and Gaelic. Such births were commonplace in farming communities where couples needed to make sure they could produce healthy children before committing themselves to marriage. Records are incomplete for the period of Macquarie's birth, but a couple with the names of his parents, Lachlan Macquarie and Margaret Mclean asked the local minister to marry them in 1768. Macquarie himself was born in 1761 after at least three other children.

About half a mile out to sea, slightly south-east of Cul a gheata is MacQuarrie's Rock which the oral traditions of 20th century Ulva liked to associate with the shipwreck of Lord Ullin's daughter (see p. 44).

A final oral tradition recorded in 1939 placed Macquarie's birthplace in a house "near the present fank." There is one conspicuous sheep enclosure, or fank, at the eastern end of the track to Gometra, a mile north of Ormaig, and another much further west, closer to Ballygartan.

Bracadale Steadings. This is the site of the ancestral home of the MacQuarrie chiefs but nothing now remains. A minor chief might have a larger house than his tenants, but it was likely to be of the same single storey construction. Extra rooms would be added to the ends in the same way that they have been added to the gabled houses at Ormaig. The open-fronted cart house beside the track would have been of appropriate size and shape before the pillared extension was brought forward and the kennels were added at the back. The chief's home appeared mean to those sophisticates from London and Edinburgh, the great English man of letters Dr Samuel Johnson and his biographer James Boswell. Forced to stay overnight in 1773, they shared a room large enough to contain two elegant beds hung with

Iona   *Little Colonsay*   *Staffa*

fashionable Indian cotton and spread with clean sheets, but the beds stood on an earth floor made muddy by October rain, which blew in through the broken windows. The two men took care to talk among themselves in Latin, since Highland walls were thin, made either of hurdles like the reconstructed internal wall of Sheila's Cottage, or of single planks. Boswell and Johnson liked their affable host and sympathised with his predicament, but they also liked their comforts. Trying to conform to these Lowland standards was helping to bankrupt the old chief and others like him. He finally lost his home and estate in 1777.

Ulva House is visible through the trees across the track from Bracadale Steadings. It is built on the site of the original Ulva House which was destroyed by fire in 1954 and is roughly of the same size and proportions. The first Ulva House was built after 1785 by Colin Macdonald of Boisdale as a spacious modern home for his family. After 1800, his son Ranald, added two substantial wings to accommodate his many visitors. From 1826 to 1835 Charles Macquarie and his family lived there and both he and his wife Marianne died in the house.

Ulva Church is one of the "parliamentary churches" authorised by an Act of Parliament in 1823. They were built in remote areas of Britain in thanksgiving for victory in the Napoleonic wars and in recognition of the many lives lost. Salen church was rebuilt under this programme at the prompting of Lachlan Macquarie while Charles Macquarie provided land on Ulva for a new church and a manse for a resident minister. The dedication to St Euan of Ardstraw appears to be a misunderstanding of the dedication of the old church at Kilvickewen.

The church was built in 1828 to a standard T-shaped Telford design but with a traditional earth floor to save money. The exterior of harled or rough-cast walls with stone detailing and latticed windows remains relatively unchanged except for the repositioning of one of the doors from the south-west to the north-east side and the addition of a boiler house with a tall chimney. Inside there has been extensive remodelling to create a community hall. A rare survival is the impressive two-tier pulpit, once a standard feature of Telford churches. From the front desk, a precentor led the unaccompanied singing, the minister preached from

Cape Pillar, Tasmania, from the west, which reminded the Macquaries of Gribun.

the main pulpit and a tall sounding board at the back projected their voices out into the body of the church. Originally, it stood in a dominant position in the centre of the south-west wall. Beside the church, stands the former manse, built to a single-storied Telford design. It has two short side wings enclosing a central block and looks out over the glebe fields where the minister could graze livestock.

Loch na Keal

The entire north shore of Loch na Keal was added to Jarvisfield estate in 1816 as part of a block of land stretching eight miles from Gruline past Ulva Ferry to a stream which marks the boundary with Lagganulva. It extended north for four miles to reach the headwaters of the Aros River. The land was bought by Charles Macquarie on his brother's behalf at a time when large sales of parts of the Duke of Argyll's estates tempted many on Mull to overreach themselves. Land bought then at inflated prices later dropped in value and proved difficult to sell.

Oskamull. Seven miles from Gruline on the B8073 to Ulva Ferry the road rounds a bend and descends past a wooden bench looking out to sea on the left. Just beyond, on the same side of the road, an unsigned track leads down to a fish farm. It is possible for a car to pull off the road and park here briefly.

Landmarks from Oskamull. The wooden bench partway up the hill gives excellent views across Loch na Keal and the Sound of Ulva. The near headland rearing up to the left is Gribun where the last chief of the MacQuarries farmed in his old age and the large, sloping island in front of it is Inchkenneth where he was buried. To the right, the long island of Ulva appears in profile. Conspicuous near its eastern end is Dun Bhioramuil, a conical volcanic hillock topped by the private burial ground of Francis William Clark, who bought Ulva in 1836 after Charles Macquarie's death.

Gribune-Head, Isle of Mull, by William Daniell, 1813

Elizabeth Macquarie's first view of Australia. On 16th December 1809, as their ship rounded Van Diemen's Land (now Tasmania) from the south-west, Elizabeth's diary records "... at eight o'clock in the morning, we saw Cape Pillar at about five miles distance. The Cape is form'd exactly like a part of Gribun [?] in the Isle of Mull opposite to Oskamull. I do not know of any place the resemblance to which would be so gratifying to me, some of the happiest days of my life being spent at Mrs Macquarie's ... house at Oskamull. The weather was too thick to admit of our seeing the Pillar at the time we look'd out, but it had been seen a few minutes before by several persons in the ship."

An 1813 view of Gribun from the north-east by William Daniell (p.43) is strikingly similar to Cape Pillar in its outlines and even transforms two great rocks on the beach into a pillar and lesser stack. It is difficult to believe that Elizabeth was not familiar with a similar artist's impression. She was an experienced sailor of small boats and may have had a good eye for coastal landscapes but she had spent little time at Oskamull from where Gribun appears as a vertical drop onto a straight, featureless slope into the sea. She may have been seeking resemblances to the MacQuarrie homelands since the columnar basalt cliffs of Tasmania's south shore, particularly at the entrance to Hobart harbour, rival those of Staffa.

"Lord Ullin's Daughter." The left hand track to the fish farm also leads to an ancient burial ground on part of the old Oskamull farm. Here the MacQuarrie Association has raised a slender, Celtic-style cross to the memory of Lord Ullin's Daughter whose elopement with a supposed MacQuarrie chief "the Lord of Ulva's isle" ended in tragedy. They set sail in a storm to escape her father's pursuit and were drowned when their boat capsized. The bodies were washed up and are thought to be buried under a flat slab in the cemetery. The story, which probably has some basis in fact, was made famous in an immensely popular poem by Thomas Campbell, who worked as a tutor on Mull in 1795. He pushed his hero and heroine up the social scale for the sake of dramatic intensity, but in real

"Come back! Come back!" he cried in grief,
"Across the stormy water:
And I'll forgive your Highland Chief,
My daughter! - O my daughter."

life the girl is thought to have been a daughter of Allan Maclean of Knock. Allan translates to Ullin when spoken in a Mull accent.

In 1819, Lachlan Macquarie wrote approvingly of his brother Charles as a possible "Lord of Ulva's Isle" when he heard that he hoped to buy Ulva, though later he backtracked when Charles asked him for the money. *The Fatal Shore*, Richard Hughes' classic 1987 account of the penal colony in New South Wales, also takes its title from the poem which is written out in full on the base of the commemorative cross.

Oskamull Farm. A stream to the east of the fish farm track marks the eastern end of the farm in Macquarie's day. Its western end is visible a few hundred yards ahead where a group of farm buildings stands to the right of the road more or less opposite a red telephone kiosk. From the shore, and the island by the fish farm, it stretches north to Cnoc Clach-na-ciste on the skyline just east of the present farm house. Six tenants shared this 75 acre farm. With the tenants of two neighbouring farms to the east – Acharonich and Acharn – they also shared about 300 acres of summer grazing land two miles away across the hills to the north.

In 1771 Betty, Lachlan Macquarie's sister and her husband Farquhar Maclaine, a carpenter, rented one sixth of the farm. In 1775, when Macquarie was 14 years old and getting an education in Edinburgh, his parents took an adjoining tenancy. His father died later that year and within a few years the three older sons had all left to fight in the American War of Independence. Though their mother was an active farmer, these communities also included cottars, usually poor relations, who lived in separate houses, paid no rent but helped the tenants with their work. The cottars were also a useful source of labour for harvesting and processing the huge quantities of seaweed required for kelp production which had become lucrative on these coastal farms.

Once Macquarie started to prosper in India, he regularly sent money home to his mother and sister and when he returned briefly in 1804 to take possession of the Jarvisfield estate, he made arrangements to enlarge and improve his mother's house. This would become the present Oskamull farmhouse, opposite the red telephone kiosk. He also engaged two servants for her since she was now about 74. She died in 1810. Farquhar Maclaine died in 1822, but Betty lived on until 1833.

It is not easy, even from estate plans, to distinguish which areas of the farm were assigned to which tenants, but in an estate survey of 1828, there is a stern observation that tenants at the west end of the property which was once occupied by Macquarie's mother and was still farmed by his sister had reduced too much land near the shore to bare rock by taking peat off it. In future it was recommended that they be required to bring fuel off the hills like their neighbours. It illustrates the hard work involved, or perhaps shirked by the well-connected in fetching home winter fuel from a distance.

The Oskamull Shielings and Glen MacQuarrie

Access. Five miles along the road from Aros to Dervaig, the forestry plantation on the left of the road gives way to open country. The stream that marks the boundary is the Allt Gleann Mhic Caraidh – the "River of the Glen MacQuarrie" and at this point it is also the western boundary of the shielings.

The Oskamull Shielings comprise about 300 acres of summer grazing shared among all the tenants of Oskamull and two other farms on the shores of Loch na Keal. They and a neighbouring shieling form the extreme northern tip of Mac-quarie's Jarvisfield estate, in a strategic position alongside one of the most important market fairgrounds of the western Highlands. Its remains lie just across the road, 250 yards back at the top of the rise.

The western edge of the shielings follows the stream for a short distance down Glen MacQuarrie then diverges due south to take in the three flat-topped rock outcrops that are prominent on the top of the ridge. It continues down the other side into a corrie, the Corean Odhar, that channels early tributaries of the River Aros into a feeder stream, the Allt an Lon Biolaireich. This curves round to form the boundary of the neighbouring shielings and the two blocks are separated by lesser streams. Though obvious natural boundaries, all these streams were vital to summer livestock with high milk yields. Activity on the shielings was centered round the production of cheese and butter and women and children lived here with the cattle over the summer. The men often went away as seasonal workers on mainland roads and canals or helped with southern harvests.

Glen MacQuarrie. This modest glen curls south-west into the hillside for about a mile. Its stream descends in a series of waterfalls, partly screened by birch trees and joins the River Bellart which runs beside the road. The Glen was not necessarily MacQuarrie territory in earlier times. It probably took its name from generations of MacQuarries who crossed from Ulva, directly over the hills and made their way down this little valley to the Tenga fairground.

Pennygown Church and Burial Ground

Pennygown church and burial ground are beside the A849 road half a mile east of Pennygown. There is a small car park. The roofless church dates from the 13th century but financial difficulties made Macquarie's uncle, Murdoch Maclaine of Lochbuie, and his predecessors truculently neglectful of their legal duty to keep it in good repair. This church and a makeshift replacement were in ruins when Mac-quarie made a persuasive case that government money available for a new church should be spent at Salen, his model village two miles away.

Set half-way along the north wall of the cemetery, is a memorial to Gillean MacLaine and Marie MacQuarrie. Marie was the oldest daughter of the last chief of the MacQuarries. Her husband, Gillean MacLaine, was the illegitimate son of the 17th chief of the Maclaines of Lochbuie and used his legal training to mislead his father into giving him a controlling interest in the estate. He then blocked all attempts of Murdoch Maclaine, the 19th chief, to consolidate and make the estate pay. Lachlan Macquarie helped four of Gillean and Marie's sons, his chief's grandsons, to get army commissions and all distinguished themselves either by soldierly deaths on the battlefield or good careers, earning their widowed mother a pension and official recognition as a "Mother of Heroes." This and her sons' exploits are recorded on her real gravestone in Warriston cemetery, Edinburgh. Behind a tall, gabled monument is the tombstone of surgeon Donald MacLaine, tenant of Callachally, who refused Macquarie use of the site for his mansion.

Pennygown Farm can be seen only from the road, uphill on the left, half a mile beyond the cemetery. It was the home of Charles Macquarie from 1811, when he retired from the army, but his wife disliked it and they spent more time at Gruline after 1815. In 1813, Charles brought the old blind chief of the MacQuarries and a daughter who cared for him to live in his household at Pennygown. The chief died there in 1818, aged about 103.

Glen Forsa

Glen Forsa is entered via a left turn off a short stretch of dual carriageway over the Forsa River. The main landmarks are visible a few steps beyond the car park but walkers can continue the whole length of the valley. The Forsa defines the south-east edge of Macquarie's Jarvisfield estate and separates it from the much smaller Glenforsa estate of his brother Charles, which extends up to the hilltops on the left. The white house that appears half a mile down the track replaced the old Kilbeg farmhouse where Macquarie provided sheltered accommodation for an elderly man and two poor female cottars who could not afford to rent land in 1808. Four miles beyond Kilbeg, looms the smooth peak of Ben Talaidh whose further slopes run down to the Lussa River at the southernmost tip of Jarvisfield. Charles' estate ended short of the Lussa on top of Sgurr Dearg.

Callachally, a stone-built farmhouse with a white extension that is visible across the fields to the west of the car park track is the site where Macquarie originally intended to build his mansion until blocked by the recalcitrant tenant with a long lease.

FURTHER READING

Cohen, Lysbeth. *Elizabeth Macquarie; her life and times* Sydney: Wentworth Books, 1979.

Currie, J. *Mull: The Island and its People.* Edinburgh: Birlinn, 2000.

Ellis, M.H. *Lachlan Macquarie; his life adventures and times.* Sydney: Angus and Robertson, 1952.

Hughes, R. *The Fatal Shore, A History of the Transportation of Convicts to Australia, 1787-1868.* London: Collins Harvill, 1987.

Macquarie University Library. *The Macquarie Room.* Available from: http:/www.lib.mq.edu.au/lmr

Munro, R.W. and Macquarrie, Alan. *Clan MacQuarrie – a history.* Auburn, Massachusetts. Privately printed, 1996.

Ritchie, John. *Lachlan Macquarie; a biography.* Melbourne University Press, 1986.

Royal Commission on the Ancient and Historical Monuments of Scotland. *Argyll: an Inventory of Monuments. Volume 3 Mull, Iona, Tiree, Coll and Northern Argyll.* Edinburgh: H.M.S.O., 1980.

The Isle of Ulva, a world apart – www.ulva.mull.com/

SOME OTHER BOOKS BY BROWN & WHITTAKER PUBLISHING:

Walking in North Mull
Walking in South Mull and Iona
Mull: Monuments and History
Mull: Natural History
Was it a Whale? A guide to the marine mammals of the Hebrides
Traditional Tales of Mull
Mull Family Names for Ancestor Hunters
Glen More, a drive through history
A Treasure Lost, the Spanish galleon in Tobermory Bay